The Art of Implementation

THE ART OF IMPLEMENTATION: HOW TO DO THINGS YOU'VE ALWAYS WANTED TO DO

Michael S. Pittman

The Art of Implementation

Unless otherwise noted. Scripture quotations used in this book are from the *New American Standard Bible* (NASB), © 1960, 1977 by the Lockman Foundation.

Other Scripture references are from the following source(s):

The King James Version of the Bible (KJV)

978-0-692-72469-9

Please send questions, comments, and concerns to:

theartofimplementation@gmail.com

The Art of Implementation

The Art of Implementation

The Art of Implementation

Contents

The Art of Implementation

INTRODUCTION

When I was writing this book, I came across a number of stories, ideas, explanations, and scenarios to incorporate into the book, not to entertain you or for my own personal enjoyment, but so that you can truly experience the Art of Implementation in your life.

In order for you to grasp a full understanding of implementation, it is imperative that I first properly define "implementation." "Implementation" is derived from the word "implement." What is interesting to note is that the word "implement" has different meanings. One is a noun, meaning "an article serving to equip; a device used in the performance of a task." The verb form of "implement" means "to carry out or accomplish; especially: to give practical effect to and ensure actual fulfillment by concrete measures: to provide instruments or means of expression for."[1] Now I could go on and on giving you synonyms and antonyms for "implementation," but for the sake of clarity I describe "implementation" as "using one's resources to deliver/receive a desired product or outcome." The beauty of the art of implementation is that this "product" could be the car you've always wanted, the raise you want, the love you want to give, the peace you need, and a litany of other things. Now, where the magic lies is that you have every component of the resource, and now you need someone to explain how to use these resources effectively to accomplish your goal.

The Art of Implementation

The art of implementation is a multi-faceted concept that involves many other principles that you as the reader may be keenly aware of. Regardless of your position on these principles, this book can and will help you do things you've always wanted to do but had no idea how you would complete the task (let alone begin the task). Now, it would be cynical of me to suggest that a 98-year-old one-legged man will be able to go and successfully play in the NBA on his 99th birthday. However, it would be highly valuable if the same man read this book and imparted this information to someone who is in an environment to take advantage of an opportunity of a lifetime within the lifetime of an opportunity. The point is that you have the ability to do whatever you desire in life, as long as you are willing to follow these principles, plus our Creator approves.

Throughout my time of self-improvement via reading, watching videos, researching, listening to speakers, personal experiences, and praying, I have found that there are certain ways of life that must be adhered to in order to achieve the desired results. Some call them "laws," others call them "principles;" regardless of what you call them, the core of the definition remains the same; they (the laws, principles, ways of life, rules, steps, and so on) must be followed to achieve that which we set out to do. For the sake of implementation, we will focus on these areas that demand obedience in order to accomplish what we want to do. One of the first mandates is that in order to implement something into the physical and tangible, we must first implement it into something that we cannot see, hear, or feel in the natural. That implementation process takes place in your mind/thoughts.

Consider the "impulse" man who flies by the seat of his pants.

> "–As a side note I need to point out that hereto I will use the word "man" throughout the rest of these analogies. Yet, every single analogy and piece of information in this book applies to women just as much as it applies to men. I will simply use the word "man" for readability purposes and nothing more."

We all either know someone like this or the impulsive man may be ourselves. As a matter of fact the "impulsive man" is the best implementer in regards to initiation! What the impulsive man needs is a process of reigning in or controlling his thoughts in order to attain order and clarity. If for some reason you cannot relate to the impulsive man, then I would like for you to consider for a second the man who cannot seem to come up with any thoughts that he could implement. He, like the "impulsive man," simply needs some guidance in his extreme thought pattern as well. Something to jumpstart his mind to get the creative juices flowing. For names' sake, let's call them "lethargic thinkers." Both men are in highly powerful areas and are

3

only lacking a "jump" or a "GPS" in their thought process to get and keep them on the right track.

Now, what if I told you that most of us are either "impulsive men" or "lethargic thinkers," and we should all be working towards operating within the happy medium of the two types of thinkers? The medium I like to refer to as IMPLEMENTORS. What's even more remarkable is that when you settle somewhere in the middle of these two extremes, you separate yourself from the majority and become the exceptional minority who are implementing their ideas to become successful. I end this introduction with a quote by Napoleon Hill: "Anyone can start but only a thoroughbred will finish".

"*In every work of genius we recognize our own rejected thoughts; they come back to us with a certain alienated majesty.*"

- Ralph Waldo Emerson"

The Art of Implementation

CHAPTER ONE

SELF-TRUTH

We start off with the first piece of implementation, which is the most valuable part. That valuable part is you. Your total essence of who you are. The way you see yourself, your personal character, and your personal health. As you already know, we are only on this earth for an average of 40-80 years (if we're lucky). From the minute you were born, "the countdown" to death began. Some people's time comes before others, but death is inevitable for all of us. Each and every one of us has dreams and ideas that we want to turn into reality, and we owe it to ourselves to make them happen or else we will die with our dreams. It is easy to see why someone walked by a graveyard and said, "Here lies the greatest inventions, ideas, and concepts." That's a very profound statement because each and every one of us at some point in our

7

lives thinks of something that is sheer brilliance, but never takes the time to implement these ideas for many reasons. A tragedy arises when we suppress these ideas, only to see them being achieved by another person. Ralph Waldo Emerson put it best:

> "In every work of genius we recognize our own rejected thoughts; they come back to us with a certain alienated majesty... Great works of art have no more affecting lessons for us than this...they teach us to abide by our spontaneous impression with good-humor inflexibility than most when the whole cry of voices is on the other side. Else, tomorrow a stranger will say with masterly good sense precisely what we have thought and felt all the time and we shall be forced to take with shame our own opinion from another."[2]

I once read that, "The majority of barriers are mental obstacles not physical impossibilities." As human beings, we harbor barriers to entry all the time. We put up walls in social interactions and we also put up walls with ourselves by preventing ourselves from doing things which may seem too tough or too time consuming. Do you want to know how to remove these barriers of greatness from within? (Say, "Yes.") Then pay close attention. In order to implement brilliance, you must get out of the way of yourself. The majority of us lack a solid physical and/or mental foundation. We sway back and forth continually along the pendulum of good, mediocre, and bad, and then (usually by accident), we touch a piece of greatness before swaying back within the realms of good, mediocre, and bad. To resolve this issue of swaying back and forth, you must first realize that there's a problem. Take five to ten minutes a day to get completely quiet and think about areas in your life that you can and need to improve on. Napoleon Hill once wrote, "An enemy discovered is an enemy half whipped."[3] If you can be true with yourself about where you can improve, then you, my friend, have begun the process of successful implementation! The truth will set you free. And let me give you a hint or piece of advice. You are lying to yourself if you put the blame on anyone but yourself for not having what you want in life.

I mentioned earlier that you must have three things; we already discussed the way you see yourself. The next is your physical health.

If you lack physical health you place physical limitations on top of mental obstacles. Your health is arguably the most valuable thing you possess. Les Brown says, "You owe it to yourself to take care of you." We place unnecessary limitations on ourselves by being physically out of shape. According to information World Health Organization via data from the Global Health Observatory in 2013, "The average life expectancy ranges anywhere from 62-79 years of age."[4] From there we can chisel away an estimated 17-21+ years to adolescent life (depending on our maturity levels). This leaves us with 44-58 years of adulthood. And of those years we must (if nothing more) sleep, eat, and utilize the bathroom. This could be an estimated five to ten years spent on daily routines. This dwindles our number down to 39-48 years of adulthood. If our health is out of order, then we unintentionally shave valuable years off our lives, which in turn shaves off time that we have to implement. Simply put, you are robbing yourself of time if you do not maintain good physical health.

The Art of Implementation

> **When preparation meets an opportunity success will follow.**

The Art of Implementation

CHAPTER TWO

PREPARATION

I n the grand scheme of implementation, preparation is highly beneficial. Benjamin Franklin once wrote that, "Failing to prepare is preparing to fail." This principle remains true in nearly every aspect of our lives. Preparation teaches us organization, no matter how large or small our task. Allow me to use a present day example of preparation. Floyd Mayweather Jr., pound for pound one of the greatest boxers of all time, is undefeated in over 50 professional fights as I write this. Many people do not like him because of his eccentric style and flashy persona. But aside from that, let's look deeper into the story of "Money Mayweather." Mr. Mayweather is no different than you and I. He goes to sleep, eats, bathes, and repeats the process over and over again like the rest of us. But where Mr. Mayweather breaks apart from the norm is in his

The Art of Implementation

preparation. He has chosen that which he wants to do and subsequently decided to devote his time and effort into preparing for success. How does he prepare for success? He goes on a strict diet, he works out multiple times a day, he surrounds himself with experts in the field of boxing, he jumps ropes millions of times, he spends countless hours sparring and pounding the punching bags. Keep in mind that he is more than likely not getting paid to train. He gets paid to perform in the ring in front of sold-out crowds of millions of people around the world because of his preparation. It must be stressed that proper preparation is the key. Had Mr. Mayweather prepared for the Tour De France and got into the ring, he would have been embarrassed by his opponents and the world would no longer pause its own agendas to watch his bouts.

The same principle of proper preparation remains true for your life. **When proper preparation meets opportunity success will follow**. Here is something practical that you can do to implement that which you set out to do. Write down what it is that you would like to do. Beneath that, write down everything you can possibly imagine that must be done to achieve your desire. There are two pages of note cards in the back of the book for you to rip out and write the following:

I will make time to achieve _____ every day.

And I realize that the more time I spend in preparation

to achieve _____ daily and use it, the quicker I will

attain my goal. This is a Principle of Life.

Signed_____

Place these note cards on your bathroom mirror, your bedroom wall, in the kitchen above the sink or on the refrigerator, on the dashboard of your vehicle (if you have one), on the TV screen, and in your pocket every day. Also, if you have a smart phone create a screen-saver/wallpaper and put it on your phone as well. But wait, remember the original list of what you desire and what must be done? Hold onto that list and put it somewhere you can easily access it.

Message for lethargic thinkers: Placing the note cards everywhere reminds you of what you truly want to achieve. And accessing your paper sheet on what it must take is your piece of your jumpstart kit to get going.

Message for impulsive thinkers: The note cards will remind you of your goal. Refer to your paper sheet often and complete the task in order from least to greatest amount of time involved for the task...

The Art of Implementation

Lofty goals are just as valuable as small goals.

The Art of Implementation

The Art of Implementation

CHAPTER THREE

GOALS

The goals you create are closely related to your aptitude for doing. You see, goals are extremely vital to your ability to be successful. If you do not have a goal, or as some like to call it, an aim, then you will be more inclined to quit whenever hard times come. And I promise you that you will receive challenging times. The lethargic thinker, impulsive thinker, and implementer always face challenges, but only the implementer faces them straight on, giving the impression that everything has been smooth and easy. If you are a lethargic or impulsive thinker (by now you're changing), you were being deceived by the successful implementers if you think life is a walk in the park for them.

It has been highly noted by a myriad of speakers and authors that goal-setting is a valuable task. Zig Ziglar, legendary motivational speaker and author, used to tell a story about a master archer. He explains how this man has a 99.9 per cent accuracy rate on hitting a bull's-eye. But Mr. Ziglar claims that he can beat the master archer ten out of ten times in getting closer to the bull's-eye. He backs up his claim by stating that he could even do it blindfolded. The only stipulation is that the master archer is blindfolded and his target is moved before he takes a shot, while Mr. Ziglar's target remains stagnant. The master archer can have the finest bow and arrow and all the equipment for successfully hitting his target, but he will fail miserably in relation to Mr. Ziglar because he has no visual of where his target is. And the same principle rings true for goals. Zig Ziglar states, "You have no shot if you have no target."[5] Think of your target and what it looks like. The more you think of your goal, the easier it becomes to achieve it. Ralph Waldo Emerson wrote, "A man is what he thinks about all day long." And the great *Book of Proverbs* states, "For as he thinketh in his heart, so is he (KJV)."

Now that I have explained goals, allow me to tell you about size. It is a well-known fact that size matters, and this fact is true for your goals as well. It is essential to have little and big goals simultaneously. Small goals give us daily victories and a sense of accomplishment for the day. Whereas big goals are more milestones of our achievements in life.

The Art of Implementation

It is with great urgency that I stress that you set both small and large goals. Too many small goals without enough big goals will make you feel like you are going in circles without achieving something substantial and worthwhile. And too many big goals with no small goals will wear you down with what seems like a constant uphill battle. I was flying back to the U.S. from Israel and I sat next to a millionaire by the name of Adam. Adam began to tell me how he built his lucrative empire in the city of Chicago. His story was quite impressive, but a point that he harped on was goals. Adam told me that too many people worry about how they are going to make their first million dollars. Adam suggested that they should be thinking of ways to make their first $100k or $10k (At the time I thought to myself that I need to figure out how to make $100 or $10). The millionaire man was stressing a point that lofty goals are fine, but do not forget about the small achievements because they ultimately lead to the major accomplishments.

The Art of Implementation

"*Where your focus goes, your energy flows.*
-Tony Robbins"

The Art of Implementation

The Art of Implementation

CHAPTER FOUR

FOCUS

R emember, implementation is multifaceted. The next principle that must be exhibited is focus. Focus is crucial to the lethargic thinkers and impulsive thinkers. As I mentioned before, the control and jumpstart are needed for these two types of thinkers. And focus gives the thinkers balance. You do yourself a huge favor when you focus on what it is that you want to achieve. As your focus increases and intensifies, things that used to be distractions no longer distract you. You will start refraining from spreading yourself too thin. Napoleon Hill describes a man of focus in his book *Law of Success* using an analogy of two men crossing a crowded and congested New York City street. The first man with a lack of focus on his destination on the other side of the sidewalk gets tossed around in the crowd, moving and sidestepping to make way for other people to walk. But the man with a destination and focus walks with his head up and moves boldly toward his destination as the crowd makes way for him. People move out of his way and he literally walks straight toward his destination. In Mr. Hill's illustration, I challenge you to think about your life. Are you the first man who makes room for others and walks aimlessly toward a random destination, or are you the man who has intensive focus and walks with a destination in sight while others make room for him?

What I found even more exciting about the illustration is that these two scenarios can be applied to your daily thought processes. If you don't have focus with your thought patterns, you will find yourself continually tossed around in the crowd of your own thoughts. On the other hand, focused thought patterns empower us to do that which we want to achieve, which for you and me is constant successful implementation.

> *"The race is not to the swift nor the battle to the strong... but the one that endures to the end."*
> *- (Ecclesiastes 9:11 NKJV; Matthew 24:13)*

The Art of Implementation

CHAPTER FIVE

SEEING BEYOND

Another key component of the Art of Implementation is seeing yourself beyond your present situation. You see, when you mentally place yourself beyond where you're at, you have won a crucial battle in the war. Most people are miserable in their jobs, marriages, school, and so on, and they are simply "doing time" as Les Brown calls it. Remember the quote by Napoleon Hill, "An enemy discovered is an enemy half whipped," and by seeing yourself beyond your present situation you have half whipped your enemy already.

When I worked in the food service division in the airlines industry, I always saw myself beyond my current situation of making $10 an hour. I used to work around 50+ hours a week and make almost enough money to pay my bills for the month. It was atrocious! But a key component that changed my life

29

was that I always saw myself beyond the food services division. I'm not running it down, but I was aware of my self-worth and I knew it was well beyond the food services division. But there was a second part of my journey to success that I had to come to realize: it was my responsibility to be faithful over a few in order to be a ruler. Sometimes in life we must go through some experiences we would rather not go through in order to arrive where we want to be. Remember that, "The race is not to the swift nor the battle to the strong... but the one that endures to the end."

(Ecclesiastes 9:11 NKJV; Matthew 24:13). Believe that you can make it through your current situations and into your own promised land! A friend of mine gave me a word of encouragement when I was going through some tough times. He told me that we can only be refined through the fire. Are you in a fire right now or do you know someone who is in one? Encourage them and/or yourself by speaking positive words into the universe.

Affirmations have the power to transcend all of our natural understanding and rationale.

The Art of Implementation

The Art of Implementation

CHAPTER SIX

AFFIRMATIONS

Implementation comes out of necessity and necessity comes from drive. This drive can come from outside sources, such as your spouse, children, community, etc., but the best form of drive is derived from within. That's why so many philosophers, clergymen, and life coaches stress that people must have a high self-image. Once you discover what drives you, your opportunities become infinite. A key component about drive is that we have multiple vehicles inside of us that we can use for the ride on seeing implementation occur in our own life. For instance, you can have drive to wash your dishes, work out, go to work, communicate with your spouse, and to do the taxes, all in one day. Did you know that you had drive in you all along? The problem with drive is that we can also be driven for things that are beneficial or detrimental in our lives. The greatest way I have found to combat negative drive is by plugging daily affirmations into my subconscious mind; affirmations that have the power to transcend all of our natural understanding and rationale. I have attached a few affirmations I use and suggest for others at the end of this chapter.

In order to implement in your life, you must first see yourself beyond your present situation. After you see yourself beyond the complacent environment, begin to write down in specific detail what you want to accomplish/implement. I once heard Les Brown state that, "Writing things down is a subjective process that engages the subconscious mind." Once you see yourself beyond complacency and write down that which you want to do, write down (in specific detail) what you must physically do to attain that which you want. Then affirm to yourself and the world, out loud, that you will do it. Speak it three times a day to yourself with the utmost belief that you can do it. Let's see what that looks like: I want to go back school = what I want. I will study for the placement exam, complete my application and apply for scholarships=How I will do it.

Suggested Affirmations:

"All things are working for my good,"[6]

"I can do all things through Christ who strengthens me,"[7]

"I will trust in the Lord with all my heart, and lean not on my own understanding, but in all my ways I will acknowledge Him."[8]

"I will be [positively] transformed by the renewing of my mind."[9]

The Art of Implementation

Focus on the next step and there will always be a path.

The Art of Implementation

CHAPTER SEVEN

DISCIPLINE

W
hen I was a young child, my mother used to drill into my sister and me a question that is absolutely imperative that we understand. Do you want to know the question? (Say "Yes.") The question she would present to us was, "How do you eat an elephant?" The answer is, one bite at a time. If, in fact, you were to truly attempt to eat an elephant, you would be completely overwhelmed by the sheer size of the animal. Well, my friends, the same holds true for implementation. Many people see the size of a task and frequently give up because it seems impossible. No matter how vast the task you want to accomplish, remember that the task will not start itself, but I can promise you that when you face your fears and take it one bite at a time, you will be further off than the one who did not start at all. President Theodore Roo-

sevelt once said, "Do what you can, with what you have, where you are." And Zig Ziglar wrote in his book, *See You At The Top,* that, "If you wait until all the lights are green before leaving home, you'll never get started on your trip to the top." It doesn't matter if you accept the analogy of the elephant or the green lights, this is a rule of life that has been established in life. Simply put, to start you must take step one. Do not become overly concerned about step 100 or step 1,000 or step 10,000. As a matter of fact, a highly successful implementer is aware of the steps down the road yet he is only concerned with the step directly in front of him. If you grasp the concept of crawl before you walk, walk before you jog, jog before you run, and run before you sprint, then you are starting to wake up in your quest to become an effective implementer. "Therefore, do not worry about tomorrow for tomorrow will worry about itself. Each day has enough trouble of its own." - Matthew 6:34.

Another component of implementation is discipline. Discipline is defined as an activity, exercise or regimen that develops or improves a skill; training. Discipline is the heart of implementing. I shall give you an example. Imagine for a second that you have a high-powered steam locomotive that, when operating at full capacity, can pull around 350,000 pounds of weight. One of the fundamental facts of steam locomotives is that once they get going they move at a constant rate. They start off slow and grind, and it may seem like nothing is moving, but as the locomotive keeps churning, the weight begins to move slowly but surely. Then, at some point the tables begin to turn. All of the initial work begins to be seen as the weight starts moving and the engine keeps working. Then, at a special point something magical happens; the train is now moving at a ridiculous pace and nothing will stop it until the conductor decides to put on the brakes.

The marvelous thing about implementation is that discipline is the locomotion that gets us going and eventually gets us moving at a nearly unstoppable rate. Discipline says to wake up when you're supposed to wake up, leave on time for your appointment, to follow through with your plans by any means necessary. This fact applies to whatever you want to accomplish in life. Once you take the first step, you must take the next step by doing whatever is required. With a written plan of what it takes to implement, discipline can help the impulsive and lethargic thinker.

The Art of Implementation

"*Our belief at the beginning of a doubtful undertaking is the one thing that ensures the successful outcome of the venture.*"

–William James

The Art of Implementation

CHAPTER EIGHT

COMPLACENCY

One of the hardest things to do in life is to walk away from comfort. Comfort can provide for our basic needs, but hinder us from our true fulfillment. As a people, when we have a roof over our head, food to eat, clothes to wear, and a consistent source of income we begin to get comfortable. There's nothing wrong with being comfortable. It is not fun to live a life of uncertainty all the time. But **comfort is the precursor to complacency**. When complacency sets in, we place ourselves in a highly dangerous area from the standpoint of implementation. Complacency hinders our ability to step out and write that book, start that workout, take a new job in a different city, and so on. If you continue doing what you're already doing you will always get what you've always gotten.

The Art of Implementation

Complacency doesn't want to ruffle any feathers. It just wants to show up and leave at the appointed time.

When I worked in the airlines industry, complacency literally wreaked havoc on people's way of life. The company I worked for provided flight benefits, 401(k), profit-sharing and healthcare. Yet with all these fabulous benefits, people walked around miserable on the job. Do you know of anyone like this in your profession?

Some folks had given up on their hopes, goals, and aspirations in exchange for comfort. And that comfort led to complacency. It was far easier to show up from 9 to 5 and then go home. The pay was slightly above average, and all employees worked full-time schedules. I worked with talented people who had the potential to be successful musicians, doctors, educators, business owners, managers, and leaders, but it was hard for me to comprehend the mindsets of those who did not aspire for more. Their complacency destroyed the opportunity to do something beyond their current predicaments in the airline industry. As a side note I must mention that some people used the position as an avenue to potentially transition into a better environment. I almost fell victim to the same culprit, until I learned to **throw away the cobwebs of complacency and trade them in for victory.** Throughout my entire life, I constantly encouraged others to pursue greater things for themselves. Yet, while I was in the airlines industry, I found I was living a hypocritical lifestyle. Here I was telling others to strive for more in their lives, but I was not doing so in mine. So, once I took the stick out of my own eye, I quit my job and began the quest to become a motivational speaker and author. And a key piece of information that inspired me to make that jump was a short writing by Dean Alfanage entitled, *My Creed*. I encourage you to add this to your "implementation" repertoire. Mr. Alfanage gives a sense of liberation to readers. Check it out:

I do not choose to be a common man,
It is my right to be uncommon ... if I can,
I seek opportunity ... not security.
I do not wish to be a kept citizen.
Humbled and dulled by having the
State look after me.
I want to take the calculated risk;
To dream and to build.
To fail and to succeed.
I refuse to barter incentive for a dole;
I prefer the challenges of life
To the guaranteed existence;
The thrill of fulfillment
To the stale calm of Utopia.
I will not trade freedom for beneficence
Nor my dignity for a handout
I will never cower before any master

Nor bend to any threat.
It is my heritage to stand erect.
Proud and unafraid;
To think and act for myself,
To enjoy the benefit of my creations
And to face the world boldly and say:
This, with God's help, I have done
All this is what it means
To be an Entrepreneur."

The Art of Implementation

> *Now these three things remain: faith, hope, and love. But the greatest of these is love.*
> *-1 Corinthians 13:13*

The Art of Implementation

CHAPTER NINE

FAITH AND LOVE

Faith and Love are two of the most powerful items given to man. Faith is a link in the art of implementation. There are two ultimatums above all other subjects within implementation, and the first is faith!

I am here to let you know that these next two items are the most powerful pieces of implementation. You can take these two items and put them to the acid test, fire test, water, suffocation, whatever you like, but at the end of it these two items will remain the end-all say-all of implementing and achieving success. These two items are love and faith.

Allow me to elaborate on each to truly show you their significance in life. Faith is your belief. As a well-informed reader, you should notice that I did not write that it is "our" or "someone's" or "theirs," but I specifically write that it is "yours."

The Art of Implementation

Because whatever you want to do in life is your prerogative. As humans, we have freewill to do what we want. Now, consequences come from our actions, albeit positive or negative, but you have the will. This same ownership of will takes form in the area of faith. When implementing, you are the only person who can achieve that which you wish to achieve. Everyone in the entire universe can believe in you, yet without faith in yourself, and ultimately a higher deity, you will feel unaccomplished and with void. Most successful people that this world has ever seen have had tremendous faith. Mother Theresa had faith in her vision for helping others. Steve Jobs had faith that he could revolutionize the computer industry. Les Brown had faith that he could change lives by speaking. Gandhi had faith that he could change people with nonviolence. Martin Luther King Jr. had faith that, "The people can get to the promised land." And Jesus Christ had enough faith to literally turn water into wine and walk on water, amongst other miracles. Faith will take you places that others say you can't go. And for implementation's sake, that is magnificent. Do you have faith in your abilities? Faith in your vision, faith in your purpose? Faith in achieving what you want to do? If yes, then you are in the fast lane. I heard Earl Nightingale mention once that 95 per cent of the world's people are spending time in occupations that they do not like. This translates to mean that only 5 per cent of the world is doing something they enjoy. I believe that this 95 per

cent of people have the urge and desire to do something different, and they even believe that they can do it, but they do not
have the faith that they can take the steps to change their lives.
Without faith, you will fall after a few short steps in implementation.

Faith goes a long way in implementation. In fact, it goes longer
than every other piece of implementation except for love. Love
conquers all. When you love what you want to achieve, each
waking moment that you invest time towards implementation is
filled with an inner peace and fire to continue on regardless of
the setbacks or drawbacks. I can give you profound quotes,
prolific comparisons, and extensive stories to get you implementing, **but without love for what you want to achieve,
your implementation process will not be entirely complete.**

A question that arises is, "If I can't implement it anymore, do I
still love it?" The answer is "Yes," if you have done everything
within yourself and others' resources, then you are successfully
implementing at your highest capacity. But beware, before you
begin to reflect, have you really done everything possible to
achieve successful implementation? If you have that love, then
the answer will more than likely instantly arrive in your mind.

The Art of Implementation

When one without foolish egotism realizes how much can be done with his wasting energies, he must carefully consider to what object will he turn his willpower.

- Russell Herman Conwell

The Art of Implementation

CHAPTER TEN

ENERGY

As we near the homestretch of implementation, I want to remind you to continue thinking creatively and write down the ideas that come to you. You must resist the urge to speed through the final pages just for the euphoric feeling of finishing a book (even if this is the first book you've ever read). On the contrary, pay very close attention to what is written and read the following pages in a tranquil state while keeping what you would like to successfully implement on your mind. This will increase that euphoric feeling, but more importantly it will give you a higher state of consciousness of successfully implementing what you want.

I have mentioned a number of points in regards to implementation, and all of them are essential. This next item is no different. Energy! Albert Einstein once wrote that, "Energy

The Art of Implementation

cannot be created or destroyed; it can only change from one form to another." If there was no energy, everything in life would be dead. Yet, since we possess energy, the question arises, "Why do we need energy? What can we do with it?" The answer is that energy accompanies constant successful implementation. If used correctly, energy is a significant catalyst in successful implementation.

To use energy correctly, we must first focus. Napoleon Hill wrote, "Until a man selects a definite purpose in life, he dissipates his energies and spreads his thoughts over so many objects and in so many different directions that they lead not to power, but to indecision and weakness."[3] Decide what you want to implement more than anything else in your life. This may take you a while. Some people have been neglecting what they truly want to do for so many years that it may take a long time to arrive at the awareness of their true desire. If you have suppressed your deepest desires for days or decades, you can still reach the point of self-enlightenment of what you want to do in life. Once you have reached the point of enlightenment on your greatest desire you are in the driver's seat of powerful implementation. You are focused. Say this phrase: "I am focused." Russell Herman Conwell wrote in his book, *What You Can Do With Your Will Power*, "When one without foolish egotism realizes how much can be done with his wasting energies, he must carefully consider to what object will he turn his willpower."

The Art of Implementation

Stop right there. Take some time to think. What is it that you truly want to do.? Even if it's for the short-term. Do not read on until you have reached a conclusion about something you want to do above everything else right now. Write down what it is at the top of this page and each of the following pages of this chapter. Do this now!

The Art of Implementation

"As soon as a man determines the goal toward which he is striving, he is in a strategic position to see and seize everything that will contribute toward that end."
- Russell Herman Conwell

The Art of Implementation

The Art of Implementation

CHAPTER ELEVEN

CENTRALIZE

The quote at the beginning of this chapter by Mr. Conwell is referring to what I like to call centralization. Now that you have written down what to do, the next objective is to funnel your energy toward the achievement of your desires. Centralization gives you the mentality of a missile operating on a GPS system. The missile is launched and goes toward the target, never forgetting the final location that was preset. The missile does not detonate until it has come in contact with the intended target. And this is precisely why one must centralize one's efforts. Steven Covey referred to it as, "Beginning with the end in mind."

Every waking second should be accomplished with a predestinated achievement. Dr. Howard Thurman said, "Life rewards the man who desires a definite purpose in life and will go even to the point of death to achieve that purpose." This, ladies and gentlemen, is true centralization that produces implementation. Many things have been created with energy. What do you want to use your centralized energy towards? Whatever it is; you have now been given a secret that only the successful are aware of and utilize. The opportunity now lies dormant in your hands. Do not let the opportunity go to waste, and thus lose on a chance to implement that which is rightfully yours. Ralph Waldo Emerson exclaims that, "Nothing is worse than being forced to see a thought that you have suppressed be successfully implemented by another (paraphrase)." And I say, pursue greatness in this short life. Inaction leads to atrophy. And nothing is worse than the cold, empty feeling of a missed opportunity cast into the wind. Why do I stress the point of pursuing greatness? Simply because it makes our transition to discipline meaningful and effective.

All human beings are being disciplined in some fashion. Albeit good or bad, positive or negative, we are disciplined. In regards to implementation, discipline is a specific strategy that is created by you! Do you recall me writing about self-truth earlier? Well, this is the part where you can take immediate action as an implementer. Good or positive discipline arises from affirmations, imaginations, and environments. Dictionary.com defines affirm as, "To state or assert positively; maintain as true."[10] If you tell yourself something is true for long enough you will begin to believe it (regardless if it is true or not). This is the power of your mind. You can literally affirm yourself into or out of an outcome. William James, the father of American psychology, once wrote that, "The greatest discovery of my generation is that human beings can alter their lives by altering their attitude of mind." Notice he mentioned alter, meaning that it could be a positive or negative alteration.

Another discipline technique to utilize is "imagination." Say the word now: "imagination." Close your eyes and imagine what it is you would like to implement. Feel, taste, and smell what it's like to be there. Incorporate as many of your senses into imagining the successful implementation of your liking. If you have trouble with this, ask yourself, "How will it feel in relation to my five senses for me to successfully implement

_____?" Fill in the blank!

Along with our imaginations, we must also be aware of our environments as they can have profound effects on our energy level as well. Someone once said that, "We listen to what's around us." And this is true regardless if you agree with it or not. You may not accept what is said around you, but you do hear it. The people around you can be an influential factor in making or breaking you. It has been repeated all throughout history that greatness has come from some type of supporting

cast. The president has his cabinet members, the champion-
ship team has their role players, musicians have producers,
authors have editors, and even Jesus Christ had disciples!
Nothing truly significant arises from one person with absolutely
zero assistance throughout the entire process. To successfully
implement major ordeals, you must have someone else with
you assisting you along the way. Even if you feel that you have
no one else at all, I would like to point out that you still have
your soul! Remember, positive energy keeps us going longer. It
keeps us charged up. Environments demand that you receive
but a piece of what it possesses. Yet all environments, regardless of their magnitude have positive and negatives in them. Do
not be drained by the negativity of an environment and/or pre-
dicament. It was Albert Einstein who wrote, "Great spirits have
always found violent opposition from mediocre minds." Do not
allow mediocre minds to continue to invade your environment
and hold you back. You owe it to yourself to change your environment. Some people may literally have no physical control
over their environment, and this is precisely the area in which
perception comes into play because, believe it or not, you can
still change your environment. Allan Bellamy was credited with
saying, "Most people let conditions control their attitude in-
stead of using their attitude to control conditions." If you
cannot do anything else with your environment you can do this,

and that's changing your environment by changing your perception and what you accept from the environment.

Place yourself in a good environment by any means necessary. I frequently tell the analogy of roses when I speak. When we see a rose grow out of concrete, we are amazed. We take pictures of the rose and post it to social media websites and share it with all of our friends. It is rare that a rose can grow out of that environment. It hardly ever happens because concrete is not a good environment for a rose to grow in. However, on the other hand, when we see dozens upon dozens of roses grow at a flower shop or a greenhouse, we do not bat an eye because it is an expectation that those roses grow and are nurtured. The roses at the flower shop are in an environment that gives them a humongous advantage to grow and blossom into beautiful roses. Give yourself every opportunity possible to grow and blossom into the person you want to become. Get rid of those negative draining environments and place yourself in more positive uplifting environments in order to give yourself more opportunities to succeed.

George Bernard Shaw, a Nobel peace prize winning playwrighter, wrote, "The people who make it in this life look around for the circumstances they want, and if they can't find them they create them." This rings true for our environments as well. Changing your perception can change your life.

The Art of Implementation

One of the best examples of perception comes from a time in one's life when someone attempts to limit us by claiming we cannot do something. We can use others' negative perceptions or pre-judgments on us to fuel our fire. That is creating a positive out of a negative. I had a chance to play NCAA Division 1 baseball on a scholarship. And before I received the scholarship, I had countless amounts of people tell me that I was not good enough and that I could not get to that level. But their negative perceptions of me and the pre-judgments they placed on me was fuel to my fire. It enabled me to go the extra mile in every avenue of my life.

Most things in life
are almost complete.

CHAPTER TWELVE

TWENTY-FIVE PER CENT

The last two steps in the art of implementation includes finishing what you have started. Nobody likes to begin a task only to quickly stop because of some limitation or constraint. To finish what you have started, to implement it, it is imperative that you comprehend the number 25. Twenty-five represents a quarter, and as we know, a quarter is a fraction of 100, which is complete and whole. Life loves quarterly living. We encounter quarterly living in our seasons with summer, spring, winter, and fall, quarterly living in the sports arena with the 1st, 2nd, 3rd and 4th quarter. And even quarterly living in the business world. I am positive that if you take the time, you would see where quarterly living takes place in your life.

Every manmade item in this world originated with thought, but it was completed in the fourth quarter. Most of the things we do in life are almost complete. Twenty-five represents the fourth quarter, the area in which ourselves and others see the final product. Most of the things we do in life are "almost complete," 75 per cent finished. We love to see people get it done in the fourth quarter – when the game is on the line, the bills are due, the deadline is tomorrow. There are numerous stories of people breaking through when they are down to their last penny, the professional athlete taking over games in the fourth quarter, and all the last minute victories wow us with the greatness that was exhibited. I argue that the first three quarters in our lives are the greatest because we haven't given life the opportunity to knock us down yet. When we first begin implementing, we haven't experienced victories or defeats, setbacks have not taken their shot at stymieing your implementation process. Yet once we are three-quarters in, we become aware that it is going to be difficult to complete and we often give up. At this stage in the game, you've experienced the setbacks life has to offer. But you should also know how to deal with them by now. We have all heard the negative comments from naysayers, we have experienced some form of doubt or disappointment; and many times we recognize that implementing is tougher than we expected. We may say to ourselves, "I didn't know it was going to be this difficult." Or, "Had I known it would take all of this, then I wouldn't have started in the first place." This is the time when greatness will manifest itself if

The Art of Implementation

you can apply what I'm going to mention First, allow me to write that every single person who has implemented something worthwhile in this world has knowingly or unknowingly been aware of this, when times got difficult in the final quarter: **you must turn up in order for things to turn out the way you want.**

Everything you put into the first three quarters must go into the fourth quarter with more dedication, determination, passion, energy, belief, preparation, and motivation to furtively complete the fourth quarter in the same way as the greatest individuals to ever walk on this earth.

> **Freely you have received,**
> **freely give.**
> **- Matthew 10:8**

The Art of Implementation

The Art of Implementation

CHAPTER THIRTEEN

CONSTANT INSPIRATION

I t is necessary that you constantly acquire indispensable pieces of information to propel you along in life. But it cannot end with constant acquisition of inspirations and motivations. You must apply what you have received from this book. Russell Herman Conwell put it like this, "The most wonderful idea is quite valueless until it is put into practical operation. The government rewards the man who first gets a patent or first puts his idea into practical use and the world does likewise." And Zig Ziglar put it in an even simpler form by stating that, "The most practical, beautiful, workable philosophy in the world won't work if you won't."5 Your life will change for the better, even if you only apply merely one concept from this entire book.

The Art of Implementation

I have devoted a massive amount of my time to write this book so that you may improve your life. I have to let you know that in life we can neither give all the time nor receive all the time. We must give *and* receive. I have been giving throughout this entire book. And now, I have a few things that I would like for you to do as a form of giving back to me. This is what I ask from you:

- That you devote at least a few minutes of your day to complete and total silence. If you believe in a creator (personally I believe in Jesus Christ), this is the time to, as Psalm 46 puts it, "Be still and know that I am God." If, however, you do not believe in an ultimate creator then you still must grasp the importance of silence. It aids in restructuring your thoughts and attaining higher clarity and focus. One of the truest quotes is by Thomas Carlyle, who said, "Silence is the element in which great things fashion themselves together."

- Re-read this book and other similar books, while making sure to always read with an open mind and notepad. I heard a man once say that, "The mind is like a parachute, it works best when it's open." Well, I believe we should throw our notepad and pen in there as well. Because we can only remember so much, but if it's written down, we can always return to our notes. Remember the ancient phrase that the dullest pencil is still keener than the sharpest mind. Additionally, since technology has advanced so much we now have the opportunity to watch videos and attend seminars to learn more. They are not substitutes, but strengtheners. Nothing can take the place of applying your own time to reading something. You become an owner of the information (not to be confused with the creator) because you invested your time to read and learn. Remember something that Mr. Ziglar wrote: "Your mind acts on what you feed it." Feed your mind nutritiously.

- Recall, when times get difficult, that Rome was not built in a day, but it *was* built! Because of consistent implementation. Small steps of consistency eventually fashion themselves into vast leaps. We all know that to increase our physical strength we must work out. You cannot reach all of your physical training goals you set in one day of working out, and coincidentally, this fact carries over to successful implementation as well. Remember that, if at first you don't succeed, you are amongst the greats! The difference lies in that they stayed persistent!

- Pursue greatness in this short life. Inaction leads to atrophy. And nothing is worse than the cold, empty feeling of a missed opportunity cast into the wind, only to be caught by someone else who was willing to put in the work to implement that which we first rightfully owned in our own mind. You have been given a new and improved insight on life, and with that insight, you have also been given a fresh blank canvas to implement on for the rest of your life. What will you do with your canvas? But more importantly, how can you assist others in attaining their own fresh canvas as well? The best way to aid others is to give! Give your time, energy, money, be a sounding board, share your experiences, and share what you have learned. Any of these items, when given at the right time, can help someone acquire their own fresh canvas. You have something great that, if you shared it, could reroute or strengthen someone on this journey called life. Marianne Williamson is famously credited for writing, "As we let our own light shine, we unconsciously give other people permission to do the same. As we are liberated from our own fear, our presence automatically liberates others." The day that you stop learning is the day that you die. And the day that you withhold giving is a day that you missed out on truly living.

NOTES

INTRODUCTION

1. "Implement." *Merriam-Webster.com*. Merriam-Webster,2016. Web. 1 April 2016.

CHAPTER ONE.

2. Ralph Waldo Emerson, *Self-Reliance*.

3. Napoleon Hill, *The Law of Success*.

4. Global Health Observatory Data 2013> Life Expectancy. "World Health Organization Gateway to health related statistics from around the world."

CHAPTER THREE.

5. Zig Ziglar, *See You At the Top* (Gretna: Pelican, 1977).

CHAPTER SIX.

6. Romans 8:28

7. Philippians 4:13

8. Proverbs 3:5

9. Romans 12:2

CHAPTER ELEVEN

10. "Affirm." *Dictionary.com*. Dictionary, 2016. Web. 1 April 2016.

The Art of Implementation

I will make time to achieve _____ every day. And I realize that the more time I spend in preparation to achieve _____ daily and use it, the quicker I will attain my goal. This is a Principle of Life.

Signed_____

I will make time to achieve _____ every day. And I realize that the more time I spend in preparation to achieve _____ daily and use it, the quicker I will attain my goal. This is a Principle of Life.

Signed_____

I will make time to achieve _____ every day. And I realize that the more time I spend in preparation to achieve _____ daily and use it, the quicker I will attain my goal. This is a Principle of Life.

Signed_____

I will make time to achieve _____ every day. And I realize that the more time I spend in preparation to achieve _____ daily and use it, the quicker I will attain my goal. This is a Principle of Life.

Signed_____

The Art of Implementation

I will make time to achieve _____ every day. And I realize that the more time I spend in preparation to achieve _____ daily and use it, the quicker I will attain my goal. This is a Principle of Life.

Signed_____

I will make time to achieve _____ every day. And I realize that the more time I spend in preparation to achieve _____ daily and use it, the quicker I will attain my goal. This is a Principle of Life.

Signed_____

I will make time to achieve _____ every day. And I realize that the more time I spend in preparation to achieve _____ daily and use it, the quicker I will attain my goal. This is a Principle of Life.

Signed_____

I will make time to achieve _____ every day. And I realize that the more time I spend in preparation to achieve _____ daily and use it, the quicker I will attain my goal. This is a Principle of Life.

Signed_____

Connect With Michael Via Social Media:

Twitter/Periscope/Instagram: @mpittman217

Facebook/YouTube: Michael S. Pittman

www.ingramcontent.com/pod-product-compliance
Lightning Source LLC
Chambersburg PA
CBHW021136020426
42331CB00005B/804